ESSENTIALS OF DISCIPLESHIP
BOOK 1

THE STARTING POINT:
YOU AND A HOLY GOD

BY MIKE AND JOANNE CHASTAIN

"And the things that you have heard from me among many witnesses,
commit these to faithful men who will be able to teach others also.
2 Timothy 2:2

WE ARE GRATEFUL TO
REV. STEPHEN SUTHERLAND,
AND ERIC AND DORITA DEIERLEIN
WHO LOVE GOD'S PEOPLE AND DESIRE THAT
THEY KNOW THE TRUTH THROUGH BIBLICAL DISCIPLESHIP.

Scripture quotations from the Holy Bible, New International Version
        Copyright 1973, 1978, 1984, International Bible Society
Scriptural quotations from The Holy Bible, English Standard Version, ©2001
        Crossway Bibles, a division of Good News Publishers ESV English Standard Version
Scriptural quotations from Nelson, Thomas, *NKJV, Holy Bible,* Thomas Nelson, 2005.
All citations from the Westminster Standards are from *The Westminster Confession of Faith.* 1646. *The Confession of Faith and Catechisms of the Orthodox Presbyterian Church*, OPC Committee on Christian Education, 2005.

ISBN: 979-8-9936028-0-6

RESOURCES AVAILABLE AT
LEGACYDISCIPLESHIP.ORG

TABLE OF CONTENTS

Disciples are everywhere. There are disciples of Confucius, Buddha, Muhammud and Sishya. There are the "Black Disciples" and "Gangster Disciples" who are street gangs in Chicago. What these disciples have in common is that they are individuals who have decided to set aside their own way of life to actively engage in knowing and following a Master. Disciples of Confucius or Buddha may want to follow the ways of these two men toward finding "wisdom" and "peace." Disciples of the street gangs want to "belong" and be a part of a group with a strong leader, even if that leader is violent and lawless. Each of them sees this Master or Leader as someone they want to learn from, be like, follow, and obey. Discipleship can be a good thing…if you follow the right Master. None of these are. But there is a Master that you should follow. There is a Master that you should want to learn from, be like, follow and obey. That Master is the Lord Jesus Christ.

This workbook is a guide to your becoming a disciple of the Lord Jesus Christ. It is the starting point for your understanding who He is and what He wants to teach you. Jesus claims to be THE way, THE truth and THE life. (John 14:6) Not a way, a truth or a life, but THE way, truth and life. Either He's lying or He is not. If he is not lying, then you will want to consider His teachings and seriously consider becoming His disciple.   As you learn from Him and about Him from His book, the Holy Bible, you will see that He is worthy of your attention, your devotion, and your worship. The more you learn about Him, the more you will see that He is worth following. There is a great saying by a godly man named Jim Elliot, who was a true disciple of Jesus Christ,

He is no fool who gives what he cannot keep
To gain what he cannot lose.

You cannot keep your life, your possessions, your position, even your soul. You are going to die, and you will take nothing with you. The Bible says in the book of Job that naked you came into this world and naked you will return. So true. So isn't it foolish to set as your highest priority, things that will pass away. Instead, Jim is encouraging you to *not* be a fool, but rather to place these things in their proper perspective. You are to give all for Christ in Whom are eternal blessings. Be a disciple of Jesus Christ. He will guide you in your career, your family, your school life, and in all things. When you set aside your own ideas of how life should be and devote yourself to knowing and following Jesus Christ as your Master because of Who He is, you will gain what you cannot lose. You will gain peace with God, and a loving relationship with the one true and living God through Him. He will direct your ways, and You will gain eternal life. Moreover, those gains once given, cannot be lost.

If reading this has sparked questions, stirred concerns, awakened curiosity—or even inspired a desire to challenge or disprove—then this workbook is for you.

In these twelve lessons, you will explore who God is and discover more about yourself. This is the starting point for anyone seeking to follow Jesus Christ. Much of the material is shared from the perspective of Mike Chastain, a faithful disciple of Jesus for over fifty years.

Mike came to know Christ while attending The Citadel, the Military College of South Carolina—a story you can read in the Appendix. It's worth the read! Now in his seventies, Mike remains a lifelong learner and devoted follower of the Lord Jesus Christ. He currently studies philosophy at a nearby university, and his wife often writes about his interactions with professors and classmates.

The lessons that follow grew out of one such conversation with a fellow student.

1. Here is a definition of a disciple of Jesus Christ. Write down the key concepts in the blanks provided

    A disciple of Jesus is one who sets aside his own way of life & devotes himself to actively engage in knowing and following Jesus as LORD/BOSS because of Who Jesus is.

    a. _____ _____ his own way of life

    b. _____ himself to _____ engage in _____
    and _____ Jesus as _____(which is the same as
    _____) because of Who Jesus _____.

2. In the Bible, Jesus claims to be the Son of God and Savior of sinners among other claims. Since the time of His making those claims, there have been people who have countered them, disagreeing with the Bible, and trying to disprove Jesus' statements. In fact, numerous cults and religions have been raised up in retort to Jesus' claims. Yet, all these claims against who Jesus is, fail to answer one simple piece of logic put forth by John Wesley in the 18th century:

    > *The Bible must be the invention of either good men or angels, bad men or devils or of God. It could not be the invention of good men or angels, for they neither would nor could make a book (the Bible) and tell lies all the time they were writing it saying, "Thus says the Lord" when it was their own invention. It could not be the invention of bad men or devils, for they could not make a book that commands all duty, forbids all sin and condemns their souls to hell for all eternity. Therefore, the Bible must be given by divine authority.*[1]

    a. Why could Jesus' claims not have been written by good men or angels?_____

    _____

    _____

    _____

    b. Why could Jesus claims not have been written by bad men or devils?_____

    _____

    _____

    _____

c. What is the basis for drawing the conclusion that Jesus' claims must be true?

_____

_____

_____

_____

3. It would be terrible to follow a false teacher and give your life as a disciple to a liar or deceiver. So, it is reasonable to ask about the source of these propositions. As a disciple of Jesus Christ, we get our information, not from a book that men wrote or made up, but from the Bible which is given to us by God and is completely and constantly true. Here are some facts that back this up:

a. The Bible is not one book, it is a collection of 66 books, written by about forty authors over a period of more than 1600 years. Yet, it has one central theme, one thread pulled through all 66 books (salvation through a redeemer), expressed in many different ways. It includes history, prophecy, poetry, biography, ethics, philosophy and science and in each of these, it is infallibly true. It would be impossible for a book to be written over that period of time with that many authors and maintain the same coherent theme and constancy, yet the Bible does.

b. Read the following New Testament verse:

And we also thank God constantly for this, that when you received the word of God, which you heard from us, you accepted it not as the word of men but as what it really is, the word of God, which is at work in you believers.

1 Thessalonians 2:13

d. The Apostle Paul, writer of the letter to the Thessalonians, was commending the Christians in the Thessalonian church for the way they received his letter. How did they receive this letter?

_____

_____

_____

_____

c. Read 2 Peter 1:20-21. *Knowing this first, that no prophecy of Scripture is of any private interpretation, for prophecy never came by the will of man, but holy men of God spoke as they were moved by the Holy Spirit.*

According to this verse, how did God write the Scriptures.

_____

_____

_____

_____

The Bible was written by God the Holy Spirit as He guided its writers, like the Apostle Paul, so that they did not make errors and wrote what God wanted. The Bible as it was written in its original languages have been faithfully copied, translated, and passed down. God has superintended the writers so that the Scriptures have been preserved without error. This inerrancy means that you can trust the Bible. It is the Word of God.

1. Blanchard, J. (2014). *Right With God*. 2014th ed. East Peoria, IL: Versa Press, Inc.,p. 2-3

NOTES/REFLECTIONS

THE CONVERSATION - PART 1

This is an actual conversation that happened between Mike Chastain and a fellow student in his classes at a local college as told to his wife. Mike is a seventy-plus-year-old college student who loves to share his love for Christ and the truth of God's Word with his classmates.

As Mike entered the classroom a little early, there was a young man already there.

"Hello, Jack!" Mike greeted him warmly. "Supper is at 6:30 on Friday."

Jack looked up and smiled. "I'll be there!"

They chatted for a minute and the conversation came around to family. Jack was surprised to learn that Mike had eight children.

"Yeah, God has been very good to me," said Mike.

"You know, I believe in God," Jack said casually.

Mike looked at his friend with a slight disarming smile, "Well, the Bible says that qualifies you to be a demon."

Jack's mouth fell open. "What?!!"

Unruffled, Mike smoothly continued, "Yeah, the Bible says that even the demons believe in God... and shudder." He paused to let it sink in. Jack was obviously taken aback.

"So let me ask you, Jack. If you were to die tonight and stand before God and He said, 'Jack, why should I let you into My heaven', what would you say?"

Jack hesitated, "I don't know! Tell me!"

"I'll tell you in just a minute, but first, think about it and give me your very best answer. Then I'll tell you what the Bible says."

He thought and said, "Well, I'm a lot better than a lot of people I know."

"And based on that you think God should let you into heaven?"

"I don't know."

"Let me ask you this. Do you think you have sinned today? Have you been selfish, or lied, or thought something that is impure?"

"Uh, yeah."

"Do you think you do that at least once a day?"

"Yeah." He hesitated. "Probably more."

"True, but let's say you sinned just once a day. That's 365 sins in a year. You're what? 20?"

"21"

Mike walked over to the white board on the near wall. "So, let's see." He wrote, "365 times 21 is ... 7665 sins. Let's say you went before the judge for speeding, and you said, 'You know, Judge, I only have 7665 tickets on my record.' Do you think the Judge would be inclined to let you off?"

Jack's eyes widened. He was beginning to see that he was not as right with God as he thought.

"God is a just Judge, Jack. He cannot overlook your sins. They must be dealt with. If you die with those sins on your account, you will have to pay for them yourself by suffering God's just punishment."

Jack was listening. Mike had his attention. He drew two opposing cliffs on the white board. He wrote "GOD" on one and "US" on the other. Then he wrote the word "SIN" between them.

"The Bible says in Isaiah 59:2, 'Your sins have separated you from your God so that he does not hear.' So God is on one side, and you are on the other. And your sins are in between, separating you from God. You are not right with God, Jack, and that is the problem."

Jack looked at Mike intently. It was clear he saw himself on that cliff.

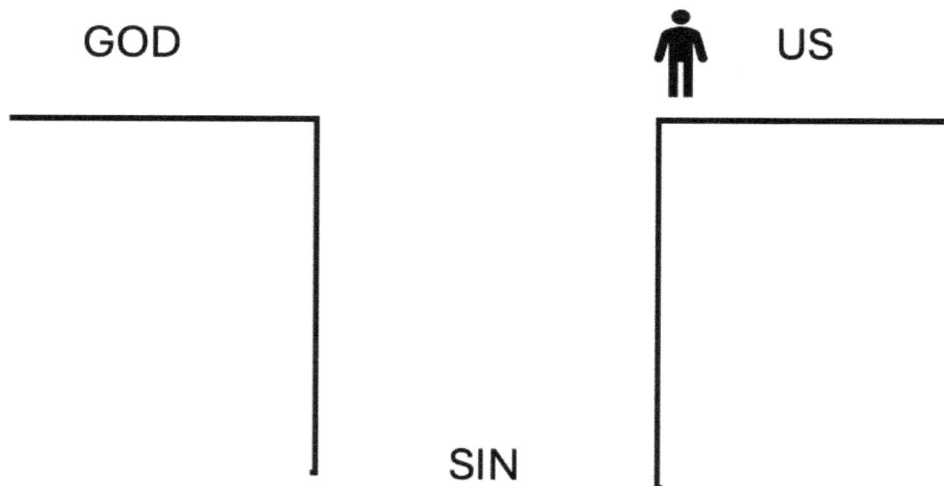

GOD   US

SIN

1. The verse that Mike quotes regarding demons is James 2:19.

    "You believe that there is one God. You do well. Even the demons believe—and tremble!"

    James was remembering times when he had been with Jesus, and they had run into men and women who were possessed by demons.

    "...two demon-possessed men coming from the tombs met [Jesus]. They were so violent that no one could pass that way. 'What do you want with us, Son of God?' they shouted.

    'Have you come here to torture us before the appointed time?'"

    Matthew 8:28-34

    a. What name did they call Jesus? _____ _____ _____. So, they recognized that Jesus was _____.

    b. Obviously, they were Jesus' enemies and expected that at a future time Jesus would exact torturous punishment on them (that would make them "tremble!") What does this demonstrate regarding simply acknowledging God; is it enough?

    _____

    _____

    c. That brings to mind the natural next question, "What does God want from us?" Interestingly enough, there is a one-word answer. What do you think it is?

    *ho*_____

2. Four times in this short conversation Mike prefaces his statements with, "The Bible says..."

    a. What does that tell you about Mike's view of the Bible? He sees it as his

    *au*_____.

    b. Read Matthew 22:29.

    "Jesus replied, "You are in error because you do not know

    the Scriptures or the power of God."

    Jesus Himself gives two reasons why we are in error. You do not know the

    _____ or the _____

    c. What does that mean? _____

    _____

    _____

    _____

d. The Bible is God's Word. God has spoken to us through the writers of Scripture and preserved those writings over time so that we can know Him accurately and know what is true.
Read 2 Timothy 3:16-17.

"All Scripture is breathed out by God and profitable for teaching, for reproof,

for correction, and for training in righteousness,

that the man of God may be complete, equipped for every good work."

Write down four things you can learn about the Bible from this verse.

_____

_____

_____

_____

_____

_____

_____

_____

3. Mike asked Jack, "If you were to die tonight and stand before God and He said, 'Why should I let you into My heaven', what would you say?" What would *you* say?

_____

_____

_____

_____

4. What does the Bible say sin does between man and God? _____

_____

_____

5. Mike tells Jack that God is a just judge and cannot overlook his sins. He illustrated that reality with the two cliffs and the chasm in between. Explain why Mike illustrated Jack's relationship with God in this way. _____

_____

_____

_____

6. Does this illustrate your relationship with God? Why or why not?

_____

_____

_____

_____

_____

_____

7. Mike told Jack about Isaiah 59:2.

    Your sins have separated you from your God so that He does not hear.

    a. From what you have learned, why does sin separate us from God?

    _____

    _____

    _____

    _____

    _____

    _____

    b. From this verse, what is the consequence of this separation? _____

    _____

    c. What does it mean that God does not hear and what are the implications of that?

    _____

    _____

    _____

    _____

    d. Do you think God hears your prayers? _____ Why or why not?

    _____

    _____

    _____

    _____

    e. Write down questions and objections that you or others may have at this point in the study.

    _____

    _____

    _____

NOTES/REFLECTIONS

THE CONVERSATION - PART 2

"But I go to church," protested Jack. "I don't hurt people. I try to be good. Why can't God just forgive my sins?" asked Jack. "Isn't that His job?"

"That's a good question," answered Mike. "And there's a good answer. It is because God would violate his own character and moral essence to do so. You see, God is holy and cannot morally accept anyone unholy in His presence."

Mike wrote "holy" on God's cliff.

"That means He is morally perfect in all He is and all He does. (Isaiah 6:3) In addition, God is just."

Mike wrote "just" on God's cliff.

"He is the holy just Judge. That means that if you are guilty, He has to declare that you are guilty." (Exodus 34:7)

Jack was intently listening, so Mike continued.

"Let's say someone stole your car, was caught, and stood before the judge admitting his guilt. Would the judge be just if he just let the guy go without any consequences, just because he wanted to?

"No, that wouldn't be fair." Jack protested. "He stole my car."

"Exactly," Mike affirmed. "A just judge would find him guilty and make sure that he paid the just penalty. So, you see, God being the perfect holy Judge, must declare someone guilty of breaking His law, if they are indeed guilty. He cannot just let us off without violating His own character. He would not be holy if He did. So, if you go to church, or you do some good, but have tens of thousands of sins on your account, can He honestly find you 'not guilty?'"

Jack was tracking.

"Jack, let's look at what the Bible says about us. Romans 3:23 says, 'All have sinned and fall short of the glory of God.' Sin is breaking God's law, so according to this verse, how many humans have broken God's law?"

"All."

"That's right. All of us have sinned. Now look at Romans 6:23, 'The wages of sin is death.' What are wages?"

"Wages, I guess that's what you earn when you work."

"Right, so this verse tells us that we all earn or deserve death because we sin. Another word for death is separation. We earn spiritual death meaning that we are separated from God like we illustrate by these two cliffs. We also earn physical death, where one day, every single person will experience separation of his soul and his body. You see, Jack, you are two parts. You have a body and a soul. One day, you will die and at that moment your body will separate from your soul."

"What happens to my soul?"

"The Bible tells us in Hebrews 9:27, 'It is appointed for a man to die once, and after that the judgment.' So, when you die, your soul immediately goes before God to be judged as to whether there is sin on your account. What will He find when you die, Jack?"

"Well not just me! Everybody! You said ALL have sinned, so that means that everyone will be found guilty!"

"You are on to something. God is perfectly just to find every single person guilty and give them the punishment they deserve, and that punishment is terrible. 2 Thessalonians 1:8-9 says, 'In flaming fire, bringing judgment on those who don't know God and on those who refuse to obey the Good News of our Lord Jesus. They will be punished with eternal destruction, forever separated from the Lord and from His glorious power.'

Mike paused to let the weight of God's Word rest on Jack's mind and heart.

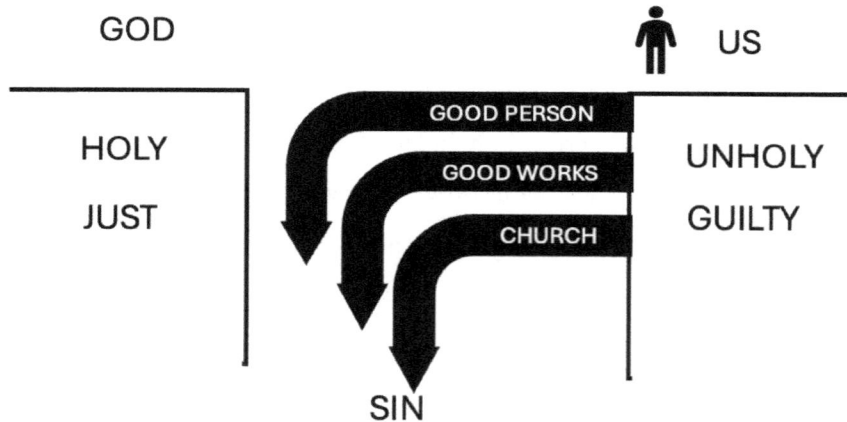

Finally, Jack said, "But that's hopeless. That means no one is right with God. Everyone is going to be punished because everyone is separated from God, and God can't do anything about it and stay true to Himself."

Mike smiled, "It's true that the situation is hopeless in terms of *our* being able to do anything. But God is great and full of love and compassion! He has provided one way for this gap to be bridged. There is only one way that maintains His holiness, keeps His justice and displays His great love and mercy.

Jack leaned in.

NOTES/REFLECTIONS

THE CHARACTER OF GOD

The character of God is Who He is. He acts and has emotions and makes decisions based in His character. God is very complex, but He is knowable because He has revealed Himself in Holy Scripture, the book that God wrote so that we may learn of Him and His ways. We are going to look at three of God's attributes or character qualities that pertain to the problem of sin and God's remedy.

1. GOD IS HOLY

    a. Isaiah 6: 3. *Holy, holy, holy is the Lord Almighty, the whole earth is full of His glory.* What main attribute is mentioned three times? _____

    b. Habakkuk 1:13a *Your eyes are too pure to approve evil, and You cannot look on wickedness with favor.* What does this tell you about the holiness of God?

        _____

        _____

    c. Revelation 15:4a *"Who will not fear, O Lord, and glorify Your name? For You alone are holy."* Who is holy besides God?

        _____

    d. Holy means that God is morally perfect and separate from all that is not morally perfect. His perfection is operative in everything He is and everything He does. He is holy in His justice. He is holy in His decision making. He is holy in every attitude and action. He can do absolutely no wrong. Psalm 98:5 *Exalt the Lord our God and worship at His footstool; holy is He.* According to this verse, what does God want you to *do* in light of His holiness?

        _____

        _____

        _____

        _____

        _____

        _____

2. GOD IS JUST

   a. Deuteronomy 32:4 *"The Rock! His work is perfect, for all His ways are just; a God of faithfulness and without injustice, righteous and upright is He."* What does this verse teach about God's justice? _____

_____

_____

_____

Psalm 7:11a *"God is an honest judge..."* Exodus 34:7 *"He does not leave the guilty unpunished..."* If a person comes before a judge, and that person is guilty, what must a just judge do?_____

_____

_____

_____

So, when *you* are brought before God, the just Judge, at the time of your death, will you be found guilty or not guilty of breaking His commands?

_____

_____

_____

3. GOD IS LOVE

   a. Psalm 86:15 *"But you, <u>Lord</u>, are a <u>compassionate</u> and <u>gracious</u> God, <u>slow to anger</u>, abounding in <u>love</u> and <u>faithfulness</u>."* God has many attributes or character qualities. These attributes drive His actions. In this verse there are six attributes or character qualities of God. List them here:

      i. _____   iv. _____

      ii. _____   v. _____

      iii. _____   vi. _____

   b. To abound is to be very plentiful, abundant, and generous. In what two attributes is God abounding? Write it and then another word that further describes it.

      i. _____ - _____

      ii. _____ - _____

   c. While God is abounding in love, His love cannot be exercised in such a way as to go against His other attributes. We have learned that God has made you and has given you a soul that can never die. You sin. You break God's commands and when you do, it is a mark against your soul. It is a crime for which you must pay. That payment will come when you die, your soul and body are separated, and your soul goes before God in heaven. If you are found guilty of sin against him (and you will be), God cannot, because of love, declare you to be not guilty. That would violate his attribute of justice. God is a just judge and will declare you guilty if indeed you are. But God is love, in fact, *abounding* in love so Psalm 86:15 tells us. This love motivated Him to provide a way for sinners to be made right with Him while at the same time, maintaining the perfection of all His attributes.

> *"This is how God showed His love among us: He sent His one and only Son into the world that we might live through Him. This is love: not that we loved God, but that He loved us and sent His Son as an atoning sacrifice for our sins."*
>
> 1 John 4:9-10

i. How does this verse tell us that God showed His love to us?

_____

_____

_____

ii. Why would God want to make people right with Him? Why would He care about humans? Look at Genesis 5:2. He **created** *them male and female, and He* **blessed** *them and* **named** *them Man in the day when they were created.*

What does this tell you about where man came from?

_____

_____

_____

He made mankind as His special creation, different from all the other creatures. This verse tells us that he created us, blessed us and named us. He gave us souls that can never die and gave us the ability, unlike the rest of creation, to be moral creatures who can communicate with Him in knowledge and understanding. God gave us some aspects of His character and as such we are made in His image. The first man and woman He made were morally perfect and had perfect fellowship with God.

Look at Isaiah 53:2. *But your iniquities have separated you from your God; and your sins have hidden His face from you, so that He will not hear.* What does this verse say our iniquities (sins) do between us and God?

_____

_____

d. That is what sin does. Sin, which is disobedience to God's commands, separates us from God.

THE CHARACTER OF MAN

Now let's look at the character of man. First, answer this question: Is there anything God cannot do? That is a trick question, because the answer is "YES!" There are many things God cannot do like... lie, change, and in general, act contrary to His character. God cannot be unholy, unjust and, thankfully for us, God cannot be unloving. But what about man? What is the character of man? God's Word reveals that too.

1. ALL HAVE SINNED

Look at Romans 3:23. "*For all have sinned and fall short of the glory of God.*" According to this verse, how many people have disobeyed God and fallen short of being able to be in the glory of His presence? _____. Is there any human then, who is without sin?
Yes   No

2. THE WAGES OF SIN IS DEATH

a. Now let's look at Romans 6:23. "*For the wages of sin is death...*". Wages are something you *earn*. When you work and you receive a paycheck at the end of the week, your boss is not being kind or generous to you by giving you your wages. No, you *earned* your paycheck by what you *did*. This is the same thing. When you sin, you *earn* the rejection from God's presence because of what you have *done*. You have sinned (disobeyed, not kept his law, done what He has commanded you *not* to do). By sinning you have earned something. What is it?

_____

b. Death is SEPARATION. When you think of death, you should think of the word "separation." You have earned death in two ways because of your sin.

i. Physical death – Like we looked at before in Ecclesiastes 12:7 "*...the dust returns to the earth as it was, and the spirit returns to God who gave it.*" One of the wages or consequences of our sin is that physically, we will all experience separation of the _____ from the _____. (see p.16) If you have ever seen someone die, you know this is true. What used to be a talking, reasoning, moving human being, lies before you still. The body is still there, but the _____ is gone. It has in physical death, separated from the soul.

ii. Spiritual death – We do not just experience physical death, but from the start, we live in a state of spiritual death, spiritual separation from God. Ephesians 2:1 *says "As for you, you were dead in your transgressions and sins."* Remembering that God is holy and all men are sinners, why does it make sense that we are spiritually dead (spiritually separated) from Him?

_____

_____

_____

_____

_____

iii. After death there is judgment

Remember Hebrews 9:27 *"And just as it is appointed for man to die once, and after that comes judgment."* When you die your physical death and your soul and body separate, your body remains in the grave and becomes dust. But not so with your soul. Your soul will immediately be judged by God as guilty of sin or not guilty of sin. As we said, the requirement to be with a perfect holy God is perfection and holiness yourself. How many of us have that? _____ (Romans 3:23) Therefore, how many of us need a solution to this, our biggest problem? _____

3. THE GUILTY WILL BE PUNISHED

Man's biggest problem is that he is sinful, will die and will be immediately found guilty of breaking God's law when he is judged. The penalty is eternal punishment, also known as "hell," as described in 2 Thessalonians 1: 8-9 *"In flaming fire, bringing judgment on those who don't know God and on those who refuse to obey the Good News of our Lord Jesus. ⁹ They will be punished with eternal destruction, forever separated from the Lord and from His glorious power.*

a. How does this verse say we will be punished if we are found guilty of sin?

_____

_____

_____

_____

_____

b. Read the following verses which describe hell.

*"Then he will say to those on his left, 'Depart from me, you who are cursed, into the **eternal fire** prepared for the devil and his angels.'"* Matthew 25:41

*"For if God did not spare angels when they sinned, but sent them to hell, putting them in **chains of darkness** to be held for judgment..."* 2 Peter 2:4

*"But as for the cowardly, the faithless, the detestable, as for murderers, the sexually immoral, sorcerers, idolaters, and all liars, their portion will be in **the lake that burns with fire and sulfur,** which is the second death."* Revelation 21:8

*"...and throw them into the blazing furnace where there will be **weeping and gnashing of teeth**."* Matthew 13:50

*"...go into hell, where the **fire never goes out**."* Mark 9:43b

*"Then they will go away **to eternal punishment**."* Matthew 25:46a

From these verses, write a concise description of what hell is like.

_____

_____

_____

_____

_____

_____

_____

_____

_____

_____

c. Mike spoke of the one way that the gap could be bridged. There is only one way that

    i.   maintains God's h_____,

    ii.   keeps His j_____

    iii. and displays His great l_____ and m_____.

NOTES/REFLECTIONS

THE CONVERSATION - PART 3

Jack had come to the proper logical conclusion that because of God's holiness and justice on the one hand, and the sinfulness of all mankind on the other, no one is right with God. Everyone deserves to be punished because everyone is separated from God. Jack had also wrongly concluded that because of God's character, God couldn't do anything about it and stay true to Himself. The situation seemed hopeless. The good news is that Mike had good news! He told Jack, "It's true that the situation is hopeless in terms of *our* being able to do anything, but God is great and full of love and compassion! He has provided one way for this gap to be rightly bridged. There is only *one way* that maintains His holiness, keeps His justice and displays His great love and mercy.

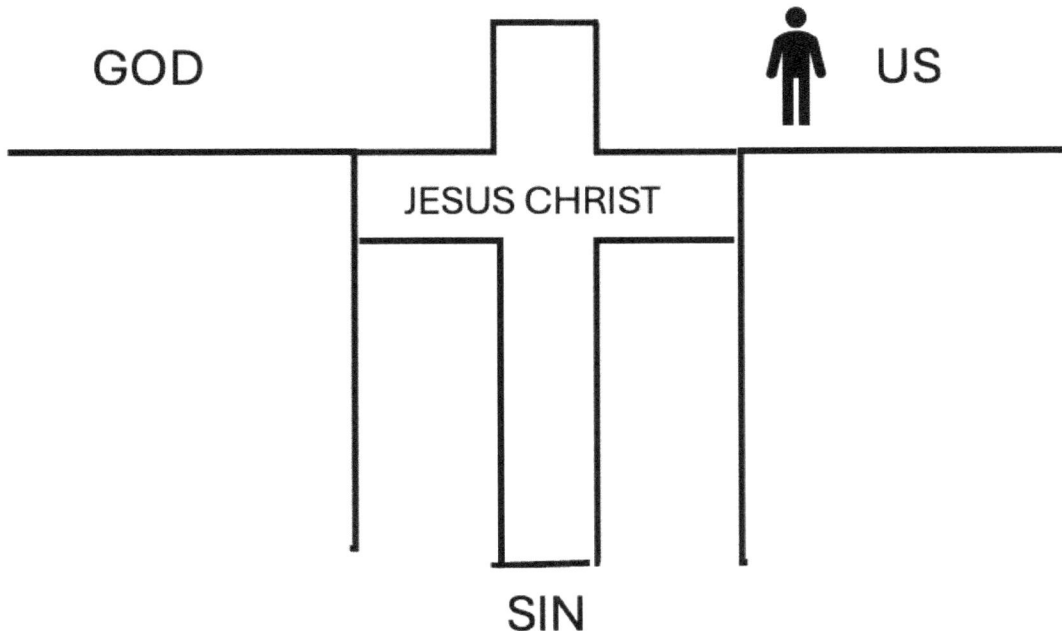

Mike drew a cross between the cliffs and wrote "Jesus Christ" on it. He explained, "Jesus is God's Son. He has always existed as God, but the Bible tells us that at a particular point in time 2000 years ago, He took on human flesh and became a man. 100% God and 100% man. Let's look at 1 Peter 3:18 to learn more about why He would do that and what He came to do.

Mike opened his Bible and placed it in front of Jack and pointed to the verse:

Christ suffered for our sins once for all time.
He never sinned, but He died for sinners
to bring you safely home to God.
He suffered physical death, but He was raised to life in the Spirit.

"So, you tell me, Jack. From the first few words in this verse answer this question, 'Why did Christ come to earth and suffer?'"

"Well, it says *'for our sins.'*"

"Exactly. The reason God sent His Son to be born a man is for the purpose of dealing with our sins. Not for *His* sins, right? Because of the next line." Mike paused.

Jack read, "*'He never sinned.'*" He looked up at Mike perplexed.

"That's really important because you see, Jack, Jesus did what we ought to have done. Jesus did what we were supposed to do. Jesus lived this life, fully human, and never sinned. Unlike us, He is holy."

Jack nodded slowly. Mike saw he was thinking so he went on.

"Then it says, 'but He died for sinners." Now remember Romans 6:23 I told you about earlier. *'The wages of sins is death.'* We earn death because we sin. Here we learn that Jesus never sinned, and yet He died. How can that be? Jesus should only have died if He had earned it through sinning, which He did not. No, Jesus died because He died *for* sinners. That means He died in their place."

"Why would He be willing to do that?" Jack exclaimed.

"Great question!" Mike agreed. "It tells us in the next phrase, *'to bring you safely home to God.'*" Mike paused to give him time to think. "It is the greatest display of selfless love and mercy that has ever been done. Jesus came in the flesh, which since He is God, is in itself humbling. He suffered in this life and yet never sinned. He then culminated his life by doing for us what we could not do for ourselves. He took on our sin and paid the price we should have had to pay. He endured God the Father's full wrath for our sin and guilt. It was terrible for Him, but it shows His amazing love!"

Jack was intently staring at the board.

Mike pointed to the Bible, and Jack looked down. "Look at the last phrase. *'He suffered physical death, but He was raised to life in the Spirit.'* Remember that the wages of sin is death. This tells us that Jesus' death was satisfactory payment to God Who is holy. It fully satisfied God's just punishment because Jesus isn't still paying for the sin, or He would still be dead, separated from His Father. No, we know that Jesus rose from the dead, demonstrating that He has provided the way for there to be a Bridge from us to God. God's wrath was satisfied. Instead of separation, there is now a way for reconciliation between God and us. The work of Jesus Christ."

"So, what happens to my sins?"

"If you believe this, then they were paid for by Jesus when He was on the cross."

"Then there is no longer a separation?"

"That's right. You are then right with God. Free to come into His presence. Free to pray and enjoy His fellowship."

"I've never heard this before! This makes sense!" exclaimed Jack.

Mike pointed to the cliffs on the board. So, if I were to draw you into this illustration, on which side would you want me to put you?"

Jack looked up at the cliffs and said, "I'm definitely on opposite side from God, but I don't want to be."

Mike loved that answer. "Then let me tell you how you can cross over. We need to count the costs."

Jesus Christ is the only One who can bridge the gap between God and man. In order to do that He had to be both God and man.

1. JESUS CHRIST IS FULLY GOD

Jesus had to be God because there is no way a mere human could endure the wrath of the Almighty and holy God. Moreover, the sacrifice offered had to be of infinite value so that the Father would accept it. Only Christ, Who is God, could be the sacrifice of infinite and eternal value to the Father so that He would be satisfied.

a. Read John 1:1.

"*In the beginning was the Word and the Word was with God and the Word was God.*"

So, the One Who already existed when the world was begun, is called the

_____. This Word was _____.

b. Now read John 1:14 a few verses later.

"*And the Word became flesh and dwelt among us, and we beheld His glory, the glory as of the only begotten of the Father, full of grace and truth.*"

The One Who is the Word, became _____, that is, became a human

and lived or _____ among us. And as He lived on earth,

men saw Him up close and could see what He was like. They saw that He was glorious, like His Father and was full of grace and truth.

c. So, Jesus Christ, the _____, Who took on flesh, was fully

_____.

2. JESUS CHRIST IS FULLY MAN

Jesus had to also be human to bridge the gap between God and man because God requires that the same human nature which has sinned should pay for sin. Man sinned against God, and it must be a person having a human nature that pays the price. Moreover, God requires that man be holy and never have sinned against Him. Therefore, the man paying for the sins of others cannot be a sinner himself.

Read Hebrews 2:17-18.

> *For this reason, He had to be made like them, fully human in every way, in order that He might become a merciful and faithful high priest in service to God, and that He might make atonement for the sins of the people.* [18] *Because He Himself suffered when He was tempted, He is able to help those who are being tempted."*

a. This verse declares that Jesus was made like us, _____

_____ in every way.

b. What is the reason Jesus did this? That He might become a _____and _____ high priest in service to God.

c. A priest is a middleman. In the Older Testament, a priest performed the sacrifices that were necessary to remind the people of God that they needed to have their sins forgiven by the shedding of blood by one who was to come. The people would come to the temple and the priest would offer the sacrifice on behalf of the worshipper. Jesus is the high priest. He is the ultimate middleman, the bridge between God and man and the One Who was being pictured symbolically in all of the animal sacrifices of the Older Testament.

d. What does this verse say is the reason that Jesus served as high priest?

_____

_____

_____

_____

e. What does the end of this verse tell us is another reason Jesus became man? _____

_____

_____

_____

_____

3. JESUS' MOTIVATION

As we learned above, Jesus is the eternal Son of God. He owed man nothing. He did not corrupt mankind, nor did He cause man to sin. He would have been perfectly just to have punished all mankind for the fact that we *want* to sin. Our very natures are bent to be selfish and to do what we want to do without regard for the God Who made us and to Whom we owe all we are and all we have.

"But" ...I love that word. Read Romans 5:8:

"But God demonstrates his own love for us in this:

While we were still sinners, Christ died for us".

a. What is God's motivation? _____

b. Define love. _____

_____

_____

_____

_____

c. What is the proof of His love? _____

_____

_____

_____

_____

_____

d. What were you when Christ died for you?

_____

_____

e. What does that tell you about God that He did not wait for you to clean yourself up or become "better" before He provided His Son to become sin and die for you?

_____

_____

_____

_____

_____

_____

_____

What should be your response to this? _____

_____

_____

How would it make you feel if you gave up something of great value to you to help someone and they rejected you? _____

_____

_____

_____

_____

4. THE WORK OF JESUS

Mike taught Jack about 1 Peter 3:18. There are four things Jesus did to accomplish salvation for
His people:

Christ suffered for our sins once for all time.
He never sinned, but He died for sinners
to bring you safely home to God.
He suffered physical death, but He was raised to life in the Spirit.

a. Christ _____ for _____. What does that

   mean?_____

   _____

   _____

b. Why is it important that Christ never sinned?_____

   _____

   _____

   _____

   _____

   _____

c. What was His purpose in coming to the earth as the God/man?_____ ____

   _____

   _____

d. Why did Jesus have to die?_____

   _____

   _____

e. Why can't someone else die for your sin?_____

_____

_____

_____

_____

f. Why was it necessary that Jesus rose from the dead?_____

_____

_____

_____

_____

THE CONVERSATION - PART 4

Mike turned the pages of the open Bible that lay before Jack and placed his finger on John 5:24.

"Jesus is speaking here. As you read the verse, I want you to listen for two conditions and three promises."

Jack nodded and read the verse:

> *Most assuredly, I say to you,*
> *he who hears My word and believes in Him who sent Me*
> *has everlasting life,*
> *and shall not come under judgment,*
> *but has passed from death into life.*

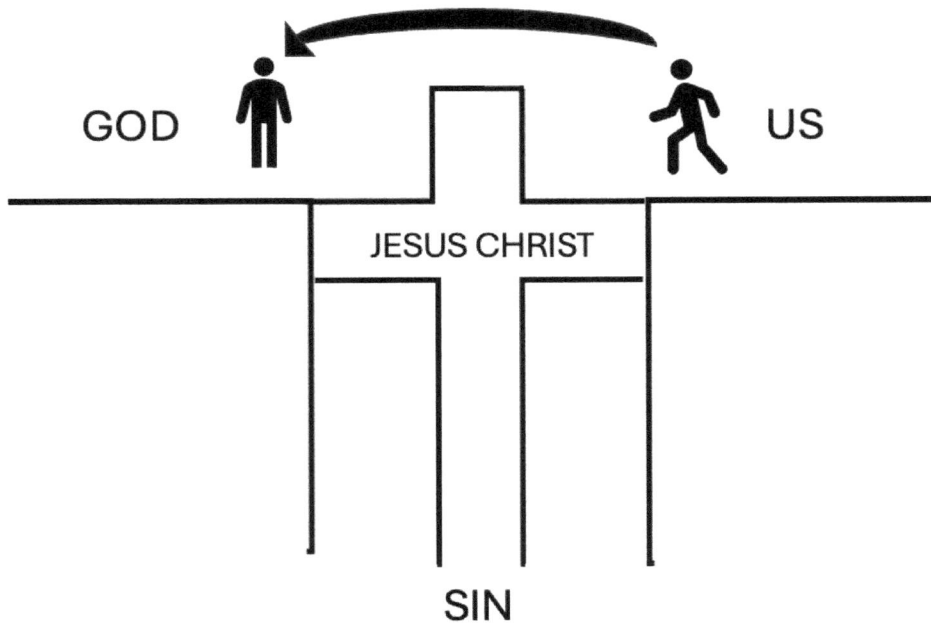

Mike explained, "Jesus says here that there are two conditions, to hear and believe. If you hear and believe, He promises three things."

"The first promise is everlasting life, as opposed to everlasting death. Remember you earn spiritual death where you are separated from God. Jesus is promising here that if you hear and believe, you will have everlasting LIFE where you are reconciled to God forever."

"The second promise is that you will not come under judgment, meaning that when you are judged, you will not be found guilty. You will not be condemned because your account is cleared. Jesus' perfect works are placed in your account in place of your sin. It's the great exchange --- your sin is placed on Jesus, and His righteousness is placed on you. When God looks at you, He sees you as holy in His sight."

Mike continued, "Thirdly, when you hear and believe, God promises that you pass from death to life. The bridge is crossed. You are then on God's side, forever in communion with Him."

Jack looked happy. "I believe what you have said." said Jack. "Does that mean that I'm right with God?"

Encouraged Mike went on, "Let's look at the two conditions again. First, you must hear His Word which is what you have done today, but secondly, you must believe. I don't mean 'believe' as in 'I believe it's going to rain' or 'I think it's going to rain.' Not at all."

Jack was listening intently.

"You know," Mike explained, "the book of John was written in Greek. The Greek word for 'believe' is *pisteuo*. It means 'to trust in, rely on and commit to.' Jesus is saying here that to have the three promises, you must trust in Him. You must trust that His work on the cross is sufficient to satisfy the justice of the Father. You can't add to it or take anything away. Does that make sense?"

Jack nodded so Mike went on.

"Secondly, you must rely on Him and what He has done for you. You must understand that you can do nothing to save yourself. Nothing at all."

Jack continued to slowly nod his head as Mike clarified these truths.

"Lastly, you must commit your life to Him. You are no longer your own; you belong to Christ. He becomes your Lord, your Boss. His Word becomes your authority, and you follow it in trust and love for Him because He has delivered you from hell and reconciled you to God."

"If I follow it, does that make me a Christian?"

"No," Mike was gentle. "Following God's commands does not make you a Christian. Nothing you do makes you right with God. The work of Christ alone makes you right with God. If you truly believe, then Christ's work applies to you, and you will want to live for Him. You will want to listen to Him and follow His will. Let me give you an illustration."

Charles Blondin carrying his manager, Harry Colcord, across Niagara Gorge on a tightrope, c. 1859. Public domain image via Wikimedia Commons.

Mike began. "This is a true story. In the mid 1800's there was a tightrope walker named Blondin. Times were tough, so to make money, he stretched a cable over 1000 feet long across Niagara Falls. He would gather people and say, 'How many of you think I can walk across Niagara Falls on this cable?' They would clap and encourage him, 'Oh yeah! You can do it! You can do it!' And he would! He would walk across and back. Then he brought out a wheelbarrow. 'How many of you think I can walk across pushing this wheelbarrow?' They got more excited. 'Oh yeah, you can do it! This is great!' He would push the wheelbarrow across and back, tottering here and there as the crowd gasped. Safely back, he would build the tension. 'OK, how many of you think I can walk across Niagara Falls with a man on my back?' The crowd would go wild, 'You can do it! You can do it!' Blondin would then look at the crowd and say, 'Who will get on?' There would be a pause, and the crowd would go silent."

Mike paused and looked at Jack.

Jack exclaimed. "That is great! I get it!"

"So, you see, that is what Jesus is saying, Jack. He can carry you over from death to life, but you must trust in *His* abilities. You must rely on *His* work. You must commit your life to *Him*."

"I can see that," said Jack.

Mike went on, "If you were on Blondin's back suspended above Niagara Falls, you would realize that your life was in Blondin's hands, right? You would have to trust in Blondin's ability and not your own. Suspended between the cliffs, you are completely dependent on the one carrying you. You will stick to him like glue! Looking down at the waters way below and the distant shelf of safety, you would trust in your deliverer, not yourself. You would listen intently for his instructions and if Blondin told you to lean left, do you think you would argue with him?"

Jack laughed, "No way!"

"Jesus wants that kind of trust because He is that deliverer. He has bridged the gap caused by sin, and He himself will take you over the gap. The infinite God has bridged the infinite chasm caused by sin. And as He carries you, He wisely and graciously gives you commands for your good. His law in the Bible tells you to lean left or lean right, and you are wise to listen. The instructions are given for your good. And if you mess up and lean right when he said left, you will quickly repent and out of respect for him and in proper fear and trust, correct your ways. The believer obeys God's Word because we trust in, rely on, and are committed to Him. A true believer repents of his sins. That means you don't do what you want to do any more. You learn to do what God wants you to do out of love, gratefulness and trust that His ways are wise."

"That makes sense." said Jack.

"So, God is calling you to recognize that this is true. To repent of your sins because you believe, and to receive this gift of life." Mike paused. "What are you thinking right now?"

"I've never heard this before," Jack admitted. "I have been going to church most of my life, but I have never heard about Jesus like this before."

Mike asked, "Are you willing to trust in, rely on and commit your life to Christ?"

"I am," Jack declared. "This makes sense to me."

Mike smiled broadly, "Then begin reading about Christ in the Gospel of John in the New Testament. That is a great place to start, and when you come over on Friday for dinner, I'll have some things to give you that will be helpful in getting you started in knowing and loving God. You know, you can pray to God now, Jack. Jesus has cleared the way so that God hears your prayers."

"Wow. Yeah, that would be great. I'll be there on Friday."

About that time some other students started filing into class talking to each other. Then they abruptly stopped. They looked a little startled as they saw the Bridge drawn on the board with Jesus Christ clearly written on the cross between the cliffs. They looked at Jack and then back at Mike, and then turned their backs and sat down. Mike looked at Jack and could see that he was uncomfortable. He laid a hand on his shoulder and prayed in his heart that Jack would be strong, and that Holy Spirit would nurture this new seed in Jack's heart.

1. In John 5: 24 there are two conditions which must be met for someone to cross over to God. What are the two conditions?

    a. _____

    b. _____

2. What does it mean to "believe?"

    a. _____

    b. _____

    c. _____

3. Describe what it is to "trust in" Christ.

    _____

    _____

    _____

    _____

4. Describe what it is to "rely on" Christ.

    _____

    _____

    _____

    _____

5. Describe what it is to "commit to" Christ.

    _____

    _____

    _____

    _____

    _____

    _____

6. What makes you right with God?

_____

_____

_____

_____

7. Mike told Jack that God was calling him to do three things. They each begin with an "R." List those here

     R_____

     R_____

     R_____

8. Firstly, God calls a man to recognize that he is a sinner and is in and of himself unable to satisfy the righteous demands of the one true and living, holy God. Write down what you recognize about God and yourself at this point in your life._____

_____

_____

_____

_____

_____

9. Secondly, God calls a man to repent. God does not tolerate "fair weather" friends. The Bible teaches that if a man truly recognizes who he is and Who God is, then he will not want to continue in his old sinful ways as a way of life any longer. When a person is given faith to trust in, rely on and commit his life to God through Jesus Christ, there is a change that takes place in the very nature of that person. He begins to want what God wants. He begins to love Him, to want to know Him and to follow His commands with joy. This is called repentance. It is a gift from God, which He gives you when He gives you faith, He also gives you an understanding of how merciful He has been to you and that causes you to grieve over and hate your sin and to flee from it. This new nature you receive comes to life in you, and you enjoy a heartfelt joy in God through Christ, and a love and delight to live according to His will by doing what He desires.

Do you have a desire to turn from your sin and follow God in new obedience? _____

_____

_____

10. Thirdly, God calls a man to receive the gift of faith. God is offering you not just eternal life, but eternal life *with Him.* *He* is the prize. He is the object of your affection, worship and devotion, if indeed you recognize His amazing work on your behalf and therefore desire to repent of your sin. You demonstrate that you want this gift by talking to God and confessing to Him what you now believe.

If you recognize that God has accomplished salvation for His people through the life, work, death and resurrection of His Son Jesus Christ, and you are willing to repent of your sins and follow God, then write a prayer to God and tell Him what you believe and what you intend to do as His follower.

_____

_____

_____

_____

_____

_____

_____

_____

_____

_____

_____

_____

_____

_____

_____

_____

_____

_____

NOTES/REFLECTIONS

Every human being has an inborn knowledge of God and His law, and God has given each and every man a conscience that tells him that God requires us to obey His law. (Romans 2:14-15). God's law is a reflection of and revealing of His character. It is good, acceptable and perfect! (Psalm 19, Romans 7:12) God gave us His law for our protection, our guidance, our good and His glory. We are all to *do* God's law, and all will be judged one day on how well we did that. Romans 3:19-20 says, "All the world will be held accountable to God."

But the dynamic of obeying God's law and doing good works is very different *before* we are saved than *after* being saved. This distinction is *crucial* to our discipleship. We need to understand how Jesus' good works have been accepted as ours by God Himself, why studying and keeping God's law is now a delight, and the means to being transformed into God's disciple. It is vitally important that you understand the Bible teaching on justification, adoption and sanctification.

JUSTIFICATION: AN ACT OF GOD'S FREE GRACE

So, how does an unforgiven person become forgiven? And how can an unrighteous person be considered righteous in the sight of a holy and righteous God? On what legal grounds could this ever happen?

Some believe that God infuses the believer with righteousness, so he has a basis to work his way to heaven. Others think that their faith resides in them, for them to conjure up and so it is dependent upon them to believe. Even others seek to do "good" and hope their "goodness" outweighs their sin or they trust in their receiving sacraments or attending church. All of these have something in common. They all believe that the application of salvation to their lives is connected to something *they do.* So, what does the Bible say is the ground and basis of God forgiving and justly declaring a sinful person as righteous?

According to the Bible, God forgives sinners based entirely on His choosing to give them faith to believe the work that Jesus did through His life, death and resurrection. Jesus' works are *imputed to* or applied to the account of the one who receives Him by faith. This *imputation* of the merit of Jesus changes their standing before the bar of God's justice and is something that happens *outside* of the believer. We are *not* made right with God because of anything in us, not by feeling a certain way or doing certain things. It is *not* the *believer's* act of faith, sincerity, effort or performance that makes us at peace with God. It is not what God does in you, but what God does *for you* objectively that saves you. That's why our being right with God is called 'an alien righteousness.' It is from outside of us. It may sound like we are nit-picking here, but we are not. It is really important that you understand that salvation is God's work from first to last, and He gets all the glory!

Again, in the letter to the Romans Paul reasons: 'For as by the one man's (Adam) disobedience the many were made sinners so by the one man's obedience (Jesus) the many will be made righteous' (Rom.5:19) Wow! A representative for the believer lives a life of perfect obedience and earns forgiveness and just standing before God for those for whom He came. His 'alien' obedience is the ground of the Christian disciple's justification. The Christian disciple thus *begins* their walk with Christ as a completely forgiven and justified person.

There is no progressive justification. It is a one-time act done by God for you, and that is crucial for the disciple to never forget throughout his life: the good works of Jesus are what merited the disciple's present and eternal favor with God. No praying, believing, repenting, obedience or self-denial of the disciple can add to or subtract from the historical, objective and perfect record of Jesus, *now* made theirs by *imputation*.

So, what is justification?

Justification is an act of God's free grace by which He pardons all our sins and accepts us as righteous in His sight, only because of the righteousness of Christ imputed to us, received by faith alone.

(Westminster Shorter Catechism in Modern English: Answer 33)

1. Read Romans 3:28

    ...we are made right with God through faith and not by obeying the law.

    a. What does it mean that we are made right with God through faith?

    _____

    _____

    _____

    _____

    _____

    b. Does this mean that after you become a Christian you do not have to obey the Bible? Before

    you answer, read John 14:21. _____

    Whoever has my commands and keeps them is the one who loves me. The one who loves me

    will be loved by my Father, and I too will love them and show myself to them.

    What should be your motivation to obey?

    _____

    _____

    _____

    _____

2. Eph.2:8-9 *'For by grace you have been saved through faith. And this is not of yourselves, it is the*

    gift of God, not a result of works so that no one may boast.'

    Write three things this verse teaches you about justification. _____

    _____

    _____

    _____

    _____

    _____

    _____

    _____

    _____

NOTES/REFLECTIONS

The goal of this workbook is to help you become a true disciple of Jesus Christ. In the coming weeks, you are going to be encouraged to learn disciplines of the Christian faith. We want to teach you to pray, read the Word, write down lessons learned, tell others of your faith, go to church, take the Lord's Supper, be baptized and much, much more. None of these can make you any more right with God than you are right now if you have been given faith to believe in Christ's work on your behalf. These wonderful things that you will learn to do *have nothing at all to do with your justification.*

You are made right with God by the work of Jesus Christ alone. Period.

Justification is an act of God's free grace by which he pardons all our sins and accepts us as righteous in His sight, only because of the righteousness of Christ imputed to us, received by faith alone.

We want you to look at the definition of justification again. Note that justification is an ACT of God. It is not a process or a journey. Your life is a journey; your justification is not. It either is or isn't. You either belong to God or you don't. Jesus said either your father is the devil or your Father is His Father. (John 8:42-44) There is not another option.

Note as well that He pardons *all* of your sins. That means the ones you committed in your youth, the ones you committed in private, the ones you committed in public, the little ones and the whoppers, the ones in your middle-aged crisis and the ones in your old age. All of them were paid for when Christ died and rose from the dead, and His righteousness was given to you at the time you were given faith. Therefore, there is nothing between you and God. The holy God can talk to you even though you are still committing some of those sins for which He died. You can talk to Him because what you *do* does *not* make you right with God; it is what Christ did. Just Christ. Not you.

That is the starting point for a disciple. All the wonderful things you are going to learn to do for God will not be to earn a place with Him, *but to please Him because you love Him.* There is a big difference.

Rejoice in your justification! Enjoy the freedom to follow God and His ways which are wiser and better than our ways. Enjoy the freedom of not being enslaved to sin any longer and having your mind enlightened in the knowledge of God though His Word. He is wonderful to know and the more you know Him the more you will love Him. More about that later.

NOTES/REFLECTIONS

1. Read Romans 5:1-5

> *Therefore, since we have been **justified by faith**, we have <u>peace with God</u> through our Lord Jesus Christ. Through him we have also obtained <u>access by faith into this grace</u> in which we stand, and we <u>rejoice in hope of the glory of God</u>. [3] Not only that, but we <u>rejoice in our suffering</u>s, knowing that suffering produces <u>endurance</u>, [4] and endurance produces <u>character</u>, and character produces <u>hope</u>, [5] and hope does not put us to shame, because <u>God's love has been poured into our hearts</u> through the <u>Holy Spirit Who has been given to us</u>.*

List nine benefits that believers enjoy because they have been justified by faith.

a. _____

b. _____

c. _____

d. _____

e. _____

f. _____

g. _____

h. _____

i. _____

Adoption is one of the most wonderful doctrines of Scripture! When you truly trust in the work of Jesus Christ to substitute Himself for your sins, everything changes! Not only are you now at peace with God and reconciled to Him, but He loves you. But God is greater than we can imagine. He doesn't stop at loving us. There are plenty of people in this world that you are at peace with and who love you who are not family. You love friends, you love teachers, and as a Christian you even love your enemies! God could have redeemed us and loved us as friends… but He did not. In an extraordinary act of love and grace, God ADOPTS you as His child! This is one of the greatest, most wonderful benefits of being a Christian!

"But to all who did receive Him, who believed in His name, He gave the right to become children of God, who were born, not of blood nor of the will of the flesh nor of the will of man, but of God."   John 1:12-13

As you learned, when you believe and receive Jesus and all He has done, you are justified. Like this verse teaches, God did this *for* you. But He did oh so much more! He gave you the right to become His child. Not a child by birth, not by lineage, not because it's something you or someone else wanted. No, you are a child of the one true and living God because He wanted *you.*

That is amazing grace because there was nothing adorable about you that would incline His heart to you. Remember Romans 5:8," But *God demonstrates His own love for us in this: While we were still sinners, Christ died for us."* God sent His Son to die for us *while we were still sinners* in rebellion against Him. That is true love. And then to take those redeemed people and not just save them, but *adopt them as His own children*, that is grace beyond comprehension.

There are several aspects to God's adoption of us that will help you understand that this doctrine is at the very *heart* of the Gospel.

1. Your adoption was very costly to God. He paid a very high price for it, the suffering and death of His own Son.

    But when the fullness of time had come, God sent forth His Son, born of woman, born under the law, to redeem those who were under the law, so that we might receive adoption as sons.   Galatians 4:4-5

2. God is showing great affection and intimacy in adopting you. He cares about how you feel about Him, that you no longer live in fear the way those who are separated from Him should feel. He wants you to come to Him the way a trusting child comes to his father and there to find comfort and care.

The Spirit you received does not make you slaves, so that you live in fear
again; rather, the Spirit you received brought about your adoption to son-
ship. And by Him we cry, "Abba, Father." The Spirit Himself testifies with
our spirit that we are God's children.

Romans 8:15-16

3. Adoption involves a legal status. We enjoy the privileges that sons and daughters have like care, protection, guidance and when we die, an inheritance kept in heaven for us.

    Now if we are children, then we are heirs—heirs of God and co-heirs
    with Christ, if indeed we share in His sufferings in order that we may also
    share in His glory.
    Romans 8:17

4. From Romans 8:17 there is another aspect to our adoption. We are now identified with and belong to the Triune God of the Bible. That means that His enemies are now our enemies and His friends our friends. You will need to stand up for Him the way you should stand up for your own family and that will mean that people will push back. You will have to suffer, because you are identified as a child of God, but so what? It's all worth it, for we will also share in His glory. God is triumphant in His plan for the world and will be glorified as the world comes under His dominion. He will receive glory for His great plan of salvation and redemption of His world and when He does, we will be there to share in His glory!

1.   Read John 10:29.

> *My Father, who has given them to Me, is greater than all;*
>
> *and no one is able to snatch them out of My Father's hand.*"

How secure is your salvation and why? _____

_____

_____

_____

_____

2.   Read Ephesians 1:5

> *In love He predestined us for adoption to sonship through Jesus Christ,*
>
> *in accordance with His pleasure and will…*"

What is God's motivation for adopting you? His *l*_____, *p*_____ and

*w*_____. What do you think it means that He *predestined* you for adoption?

_____

_____

_____

_____

3.   Some may say, "Isn't God the father of everyone and aren't all men brothers?" Read John 8:42-44a and write your answer.

> *Jesus said to them, "If God were your Father, you would love me, for I have come*
>
> *here from God. I have not come on my own; God sent me. [43] Why is my language*
>
> *not clear to you? Because you are unable to hear what I say. [44] You belong to your*
>
> *father, the devil, and you want to carry out your father's desires.*

_____

_____

_____

_____

_____

_____

_____

_____

NOTES/REFLECTIONS

You would respond differently to a dictator or a slave master than you do to a father. Think about a good father. What is he like? Off the top of your head, what are some of the characteristics that come to mind when you think of the perfect father?

Strong, patient, compassionate, gently leads, wise, honest, supportive, provides well, dependable, shows unconditional love, forgiving, protects, spends time with his children, teaches, loves, and disciplines his children wisely and well.

Every one of those characteristics describes the relationship that God has as the Father of those whom He justifies through His Son. A Christian enjoys these wonderful benefits of a perfect Father Who will never let him down. Christians are truly loved and accepted. They are bought at a great price, and they are most precious to God. These realities will shape and direct the disciple for the rest of his life.

And a disciple will be full of questions, such as: Why was I adopted? With God not needing anything, or any attraction in me, why did God choose many like me to be in His family (Eph.1:3-6)? Does God have a higher goal for my adoption than saving me from Satan's family and hell? All of these questions have good answers. Be encouraged, Child of God, as you read 2 Peter 1:3:

By His divine power, God has given us everything we need for living a godly life. We have received all of this by coming to know Him, the One who called us to Himself by means of His marvelous glory and excellence.

See your Father is looking out for you, providing for you and equipping you for being a child fit for having God as your Father and Jesus your brother. He is giving you "everything [you] need for living a godly life."

Now that you have been bought with such a great price by One who loves and cares for you, what are you supposed to do with this life? You now have a new **purpose**. Note that God has given us everything we need to live *a godly life.* A true disciple of Jesus Christ will no longer live in disobedience to God's wise law. That would be foolish. Our purpose now is to please and glorify God.

God's law is a reflection of His character, and we want to be like Him. Our attitude towards God's law changes such that it is not the "gotcha", that is, the list of how you have *failed.* Instead, God's law becomes your delight. You love doing what He wants because you trust Him that He is wise and has your best interest in mind like a good Father would.

NOTES/REFLECTIONS

1. How do you treat a good Father?

    a. You *respect* Him.

    > *You alone are God.*
    >
    > *Teach me Your ways, O LORD,*
    >
    > *that I may live according to Your truth!*
    >
    > *Grant me purity of heart,*
    >
    > *so that I may honor You.*
    >
    > *Psalm 86:11*

    What are some of the ways that this verse teaches us to do that? _____

    _____

    _____

    _____

    _____

    _____

    b. Another thing you do is *talk* to Him.

    > *Pray like this: Our Father in heaven, may Your name be kept holy.*
    > *Matthew 6:5*

    > *Then you will call on Me and come and pray to Me, and I will listen to you. [13] You will*
    > *seek Me and find me when you seek Me with all your heart.*
    > *Jeremiah 29:12-13*

    > *Do not be anxious about anything, but in every situation, by prayer and petition, with thanks-*
    > *giving, present your requests to God.*
    > *Philippians 4:6*

    What do these verses teach you about praying to God? _____

    _____

    _____

    _____

    _____

    _____

This is a whole new world for the Christian disciple! You are not separated from God, but united to Him in Christ. You can now talk to him, and He hears you! Moreover, He wants you to talk to Him, to share your thoughts and feelings, to hear your burdens, to rejoice in your successes. He doesn't want your formalism. You don't talk to your earthly father like you are reading a letter to the insurance company! No, you *converse* with Him as One you love and trust and share your life with Him.

c. You *listen* to him. You go to him for guidance and trust that what he tells you is good because he loves you and wants what is best for you.

> *Trust in the Lord with all your heart,*
> *And lean not on your own understanding;*
> *⁶ In all your ways acknowledge Him,*
> *And He shall direct your paths.*
> *Proverbs 3:5-6*

What does this verse teach about God's guidance? _____

_____

_____

_____

_____

_____

_____

This is a whole new world for the Christian disciple! You are now *not* separated from God but united to Him in Christ. You can now talk to him and ask Him to give you wisdom and guidance. God knows all things, so He is able to direct your paths. But He wants to be asked. He wants you to look for His point of view in all things because His point of view is good and right.

Write a prayer asking for God's guidance. _____

_____

_____

_____

_____

_____

d. You *accept his discipline.* Look at Hebrews 12:5-11.

> *"And have you forgotten the encouraging words God spoke to you as his children? He said,*
>
> > *'My child, don't make light of the Lord's discipline*
> > *and don't give up when He corrects you.*
> > *⁶ For the Lord disciplines those He loves,*
> > *and He punishes each one He accepts as his child.'*
>
> *⁷ As you endure this divine discipline, remember that God is treating you as His own children. Who ever heard of a child who is never disciplined by its father? ⁸ If God doesn't discipline you as He does all of his children, it means that you are illegitimate and are not really His children at all. ⁹ Since we respected our earthly fathers who disciplined us, shouldn't we submit even more to the discipline of the Father of our spirits, and live forever?*
>
> *¹⁰ For our earthly fathers disciplined us for a few years, doing the best they knew how. But God's discipline is always good for us, so that we might share in His holiness. ¹¹ No discipline is enjoyable while it is happening—it's painful! But afterward there will be a peaceful harvest of right living for those who are trained in this way."*

From this verse, what does it look like for a good Father to discipline you and what good will it bring to you? _____

_____

_____

_____

_____

_____

_____

_____

_____

_____

2. God knows that we are going to struggle in following Him and so He has made provision for that.

Read Romans 8:26:

> *And the Holy Spirit helps us in our weakness. For example, we don't know what God wants*
> *us to pray for. But the Holy Spirit prays for us*
> *with groanings that cannot be expressed in words.*
>
> *Romans 8:26*

What does Romans 8:26 tell us about the provision for our struggles?

_____

_____

_____

_____

_____

_____

_____

_____

_____

_____

_____

NOTES/REFLECTIONS

We have talked about justification being a *precursor* to discipleship, meaning that you cannot be a disciple of Jesus Christ until you have faith in His saving work on your behalf. Until you are right with God through Christ's substitutionary work, the "good" things you do like pray, go to church, serve others, even tell the Gospel to others, is useless. They will be done as a means of vainly trying to earn spiritual status rather than as a response to the grace of God. So, before you can be a disciple of Christ, you must first be justified by Him.

Adoption is the *entry* into discipleship. When you trust in Christ's work and not your own to make you right with God, you are then accepted by God and adopted by Him as His child. (Amazing!) This is your entry point into discipleship because all the works we do after we are adopted are not to *appease* the Father, but to *please* the Father. As His child, our motivation for obeying is to please Him because we are grateful sons and daughters who trust Him and long to please and follow Him.

After you are justified and adopted, you then begin your *journey* of discipleship. Justification and adoption are acts of God. You do not cooperate with them; they are done to you and for you. Sanctification has some differences. Sanctification is a *work* of God's unmerited favor in your life, where He renews your nature to be more like Himself and enables you to more and more die to sin and live to righteousness because He has given the third person of the Trinity, God the Holy Spirit, to live inside of you, enlightening your mind and changing your heart and will. You are called by God to cooperate with this as He is directing and orchestrating this in your life.

Sanctification is the *process* of your becoming more and more like God in character and conduct. When you are justified you do not immediately stop sinning. Christ has paid for all the sins you have committed, commit now and will commit in the future, but you do not immediately become holy in practice. You are judicially and legally holy because of Christ's holiness imputed to your account. but in your day-to-day life, you are now in process of conforming more and more to the will of God and turning away from sin and toward Him in trust.

God has given you tools to do this and that is the basis for the rest of the discipleship process. You are given means by which to learn to grow in your love for, knowledge of, understanding of, and wisdom to apply God's truth in your life so that you live for Him. These studies will teach you to pray, to study God's Word, memorize it and use it as a weapon of mass *instruction* so that God will be glorified, and the earth will be filled with the knowledge of His glory as the waters cover the sea! (Habakkuk 2: 14)

As a last warning, it's important to understand that

profession of faith does not always mean possession of real faith.

Just because you have professed faith in Christ does not mean that you have real faith. Real faith is borne out or proved by how you live. If you are a true Christian, you will seek to obey your true Father. You will love Him and seek to grow in knowledge, understanding and wisdom of His ways. You will feel conviction when you fail Him, and you will seek forgiveness because you hate that you displeased Him. Remember always that you do nothing to achieve salvation, not even believe. God gives you that and you demonstrate it. With sanctification, the works that you do for God simply demonstrate whether or not you are a Christian. An apple tree will grow apples. If it produces pears, it is *not an apple tree.* If you call yourself God's child and you are, for example, having sex outside of marriage, then you are probably professing and not possessing. If you are God's, you will obey His Word and love what He loves, hate what He hates and forsakes what He tells you to forsake. So, do not put any confidence in your *profession of faith.* Rather, live as a child of God and "let your light so shine before men that they will see your good works and glorify your Father Who is in heaven." (Matthew 5:16)

The disciple wants to become like their Father in heaven. It is a part of his new nature. He received the Holy Spirit when he believed (Eph.1:13) and God will work grateful and glad obedience in them. Yes, he still sins (though that sin is paid in full by Christ (1 Jn.1:8-9)), but he will grow more and more to hate that sin because it displeases his Father, and he will more and more see the harm it does to himself and others, because His law is wise and good. The disciple will learn that his Bible is the most treasured gift he possesses, and God will guide him with increased certainty as he uses it to grow in sanctification.

1.   The Bible uses sanctification as the thermometer to tell if someone is a Christian or not. Read Jesus' heavy words in Matthew 7:17-20:

"Even so, every good tree bears good fruit, but a bad tree bears bad fruit. ¹⁸ A good tree cannot bear bad fruit, nor can a bad tree bear good fruit. ¹⁹ Every tree that does not bear good fruit is cut down and thrown into the fire. ²⁰ Therefore by their fruits you will know them.'

So, Jesus is telling us to judge! That's right, but not by our own standards, but by His Word. What did Jesus mean for us to do when He says we will "know them" and what are we supposed to do with that information? _____

_____

_____

_____

_____

Do you have any bad fruit that you need to get rid of? List it here and pray and ask the Father to help you. _____

_____

_____

_____

2.   The disciple must make every effort to grow. The disciple is repeatedly challenged to take sides at heart level in the fight. In Ephesians 5:20-24, God says:

> *That, however, is not the way of life you learned ²¹ when you heard about Christ and were taught in Him in accordance with the truth that is in Jesus. ²² You were taught, with regard to your former way of life, to put off your old self, which is being corrupted by its deceitful desires; ²³ to be made new in the attitude of your minds;²⁴ and to put on the new self, created to be like God in true righteousness and holiness.*

a. What did the Apostle Paul teach the Ephesians to do with their old ways   before knowing Christ? PUT _____

b. What did he teach them to do with their new self which was to be like God in true   right-eousness and holiness? PUT _____

3. Reading further down the same passage, Paul gets specific about what the Christians are to PUT OFF and PUT ON. Read through the passage and write in the proper category what is to be put off and put on.

> Therefore, having put away falsehood, let each one of you speak the truth with his neighbor, for we are members one of another. [26] Be angry and do not sin; do not let the sun go down on your anger, [27] and give no opportunity to the devil. [28] Let the thief no longer steal, but rather let him labor, doing honest work with his own hands, so that he may have something to share with anyone in need. [29] Let no corrupting talk come out of your mouths, but only such as is good for building up, as fits the occasion, that it may give grace to those who hear. [30] And do not grieve the Holy Spirit of God, by Whom you were sealed for the day of redemption. [31] Let all bitterness and wrath and anger and clamor and slander be put away from you, along with all malice. [32] Be kind to one another, tenderhearted, forgiving one another, as God in Christ forgave you.

PUT OFF   PUT ON

Sanctification provides the serious analysis that lip profession demands.

> *"So, dear brothers and sisters, work hard to prove that you really are*
> *among those God has called and chosen. Do these things,*
> *and you will never fall away."*
>
> 2 Peter 1:10

Peter is not saying that you can "fall away" from God or lose your salvation. No, he is saying that there is danger that the professing believers who look like they are Christians, will prove by disobedience that they are not and "fall away" from their apparent profession by proving they have no "possession."

Good works performed by the disciple before or after becoming a Christian have NOTHING TO DO WITH THE SAVING FAVOR OF GOD; but the ongoing practicing of evil as a way of life can show that Christ has *not* saved you. The Bible has some very direct words on this matter:

1 John 2:3-6 says:

> *"We know that we have come to know Him if we keep His commands. ⁴ Whoever says,*
> *"I know him," but does not do what He commands is a liar, and the truth is not in that*
> *person. ⁵ But if anyone obeys His word, love for God is truly made complete in them. This*
> *is how we know we are in Him: ⁶ Whoever claims to live in him must live as Jesus did."*

How did Jesus live? He had a heart's desire to live according to the Word in order to please and do the will of the Father. Granted He was perfect in His obedience, and we will not be in this life, but we are to be like Him in our desire to obey the will of the Father.

Thomas Chalmers was a godly man in the 1800's who wrote on "The expulsive power of a new affection." He makes the case for the fact that the more we love Christ, the more that love displaces and expels the sin that resides in us. It is much like putting pebbles in a glass of water. The more pebbles you place in the glass the more water is displaced and pours out of the glass. As we live more and more for Christ and in keeping with God's Word, the sin in our hearts is displaced and replaced with love that motivates us to do good. When saved through faith in Christ, our sensibilities are awakened to a whole new range of reality, like a new-born baby.

Sanctification is a process where, as God's grace works in our hearts, previous loves, thought patterns, habits, priorities and practices move to the periphery, and then out of the life of the disciple completely. Other good habits are drawn in, and some are new altogether. God's Word and Spirit reorders and properly locates our affections which will bring holiness, happiness and holistic wellbeing.

Be encouraged in your sanctification. God is doing it. He promises. Look at Philippians 1:6:

> *"And I am certain that God, who began the good work within you, will continue His work until it is finally finished on the day when Christ Jesus returns.*

> *Philippians 1:6*

NOTES/REFLECTIONS

1. Use the concentric circles in the illustration to help you visualize your present state of sanctification. The heart in the center is yours. Be honest in your evaluation of yourself and write things from the box into the circles according to how you view them in your life right now. In the next illustration, write where you want them to be. Feel free to add to the items in the box

distant

close

MY LIFE
NOW

God, lust, prayer, coveting, family, obscenity, God's law, jealousy, Bible study, selfish ambition, education, Church, pornography, grace, mercy, career, sloth, righteousness, faith, self-success, fitness, possessions, Alcohol, money, etc.

distant

close

MY LIFE
AS I WANT
IT TO BE

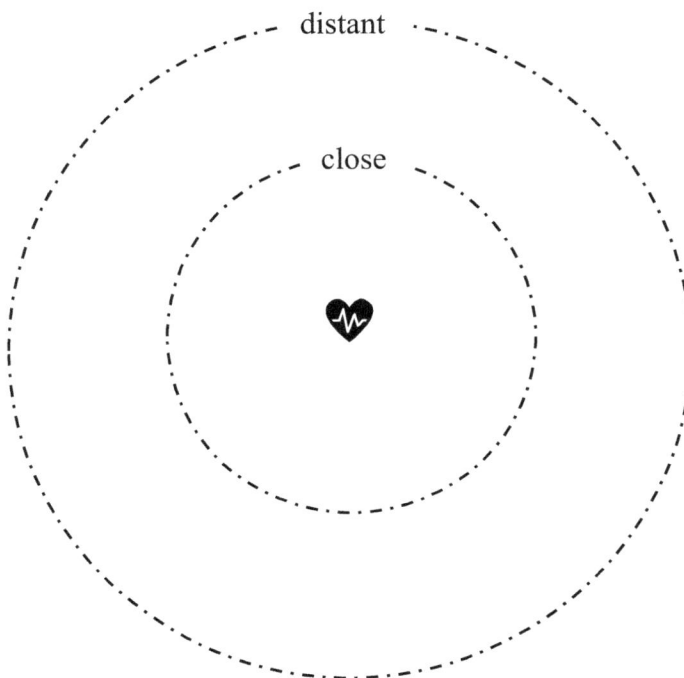

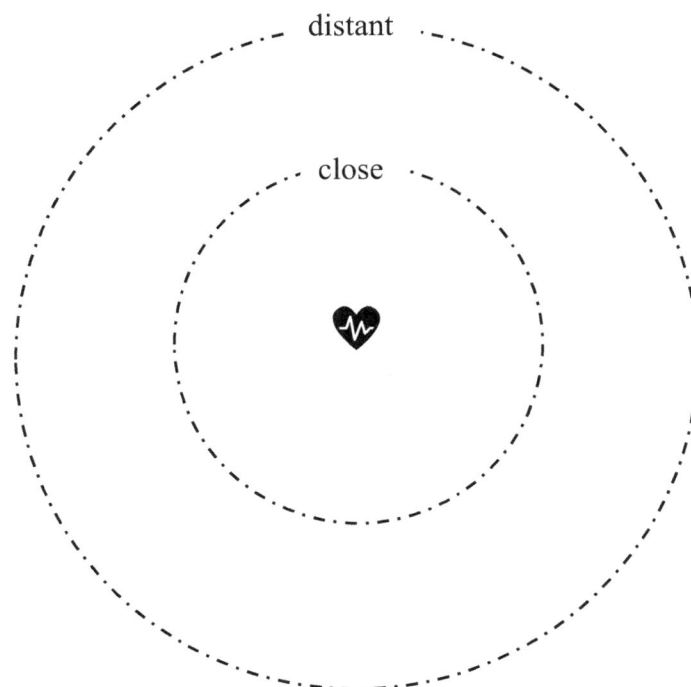

77

NOTES/REFLECTIONS

LESSON 12:   A QUIZ ON SALVATION

Every human's greatest problem is that he is separated from God because of his sin. God has provided one way for lost sinners to be reconciled to Him and has provided that way Himself. The Lord Jesus Christ is the solution to our greatest problem. But how well do you know the particular truths of salvation from the false? This quiz will help you discern that. Read each statement and circle whether it is true or false.

1. God's work of salvation depends upon all three persons of the Trinity.

    True   False

2. There has only been one human who was not a sinner and that person is Jesus.

    True   False

3. Every human who has been born needs to be saved from the wrath of God except for Jesus.

    True   False

4. With sufficient time and effort, we could change ourselves so God would save us from His wrath.

    True   False

5. Every sinner will be saved in the end because God is a God of love.

    True   False

6. Jesus voluntarily substituted Himself for the sinners the Father chose to save and bore the wrath of God in their place.

    True   False

7. A sinner must pray the "sinner's prayer" in order to be saved.

    True   False

8. A sinner must repent of his sins if he is saved.

    True   False

9. A sinner must be born again (or regenerated) to be saved.

    True   False

10. The Holy Spirit regenerates or makes a human born again when and where He pleases.

    True   False

11. A person can lose his saving faith if he commits a grievous sin.

    True   False

12. A truly saved person never waivers or doubts his salvation.

    True   False

13. True faith is always accompanied by good works.

    True   False

14. In justification, God starts sinners on a path to salvation.

    True   False

15. In justification, God declares sinners legally righteous.

    True   False

16. Justification includes the forgiveness of sin.

    True   False

17. For God to justify sinners, His just wrath against them must be satisfied.

    True   False

18. The legal basis for a sinner's justification is the good works the Holy Spirit produces in within them.

    True   False

19. The legal basis for a sinners justification is their faith.

    True   False

20. The legal basis for a sinner's justification is Christ's righteous life and obedient death applied to their account (imputed to them.)

    True   False

21. Those who are justified are adopted by God and become His children.

    True   False

22. After sinners are regenerated and justified, the Holy Spirit continues to work in them to make them more and more like Christ.

    True   False

23. Becoming holy is a matter of letting go of all effort and letting the Spirit do his work in you. them.

    True   False

24. Because the Holy Spirit is in the justified person producing Christlikeness, it is possible for a person to become perfectly righteous in this life.

    True   False

25. Baptism is a guarantee of a believer's final salvation.

    True   False

26. Only Christ's good works put to our account allows us to enter heaven.

    True   False

27. After salvation, we are required to be obedient to God by following His commands in order to keep our salvation.

    True   False

28. A disciple is one who is justified and does good works to please His Father.

    True   False

29. We show our love for God by obeying Him according to the Bible.

    True   False

30. When a person is given faith and is justified, he is then adopted by God as His child and is set on a path of living to please God by obedience to His law.

    True   False

BUT GOD DEMONSTRATES HIS OWN LOVE FOR US IN THIS: WHILE WE WERE STILL SINNERS, CHRIST DIED FOR US.

ROMANS 5:8

1. *True.* The Father planned or anticipated our salvation, the Son accomplished it, and the Holy Spirit applies it to us. Eph.1:3-14, 2:4-9, Jn.3:5.

2. *True.* Jesus was born of the virgin, Mary, and did not have original sin. He is the only human who was born without sin and never sinned in this life. Lk.1:35.

3. *True.* The wrath of God is poured out against all sinners. All men have sinned except Jesus, so God's wrath is justly deserved by all but Jesus. Rom.3:23.

4. *False.* Time does not have the capacity to change the fact of sin on the accounts of all men. God is holy and cannot tolerate unholiness in His presence. Therefore, no matter how much time and effort we use to try to make ourselves acceptable to God, we cannot make our account perfect as God deserves. Rom.3:20.

5. *False.* God is love, but He is also the God of justice. Every sinner who trusts in Christ alone will be saved in the end. Jn.3:36.

6. *True.* Jesus took the punishment we deserved, bearing the wrath of God against sin. Matt.26: 39, 42.

7. *False.* We add nothing to the work of Christ to save sinners. Only His work is sufficient to satisfy God's just wrath, so even the work of praying the sinner's prayer is not part of God saving sinners. It is appropriate for sinners who come to have faith to pray and ask forgiveness for their sins, but praying is an outworking of the salvation you are already given. Jn.19:30.

8. *True.* If a sinner is truly saved, he will demonstrate that by a life of repentance where he turns from His sins and lives for God. Col.3:5, 8.

9. *True.* Because all men are spiritually dead, God must raise them from the dead by regenerating them before they are capable of receiving the gift of faith. Eph.2:1-7.

10. *True.* John 3 tells us that the Holy Spirit working as He wills as the third person of the Trinity changes a person's heart by making him a new creature in Christ. Jn.3:8.

11. *False.* True faith means you have been justified, that is that Christ's perfection has been placed to your account, paying for even grievous sins you may do. 2.Cor.5:21, 1 Jn.1:9.

12. *False.* Even the sin of wavering in your faith is paid for by Christ. Temptation may cause a Christian to question or doubt, but he cannot lose his salvation. The Holy Spirit will bring about restoration. Lk.22:54ff.

13. *True.* If you are a Christian, that is, your sins are fully paid for by him, then you have a change of heart that views yourself as a child of God and He gives you a desire to live for and please Him by obeying Him. These good works will be the life a true believer. Jms.2:26.

14. *False.* In justification, a sinner is made righteous because of the perfection of Christ being placed to his account. That means that all of his sins are paid for completely, so there is no path to salvation other than Jesus' life and death. Salvation is applied at the time of justification. Rom.4:24f.

15. *True.* At the time of justification, Christ's perfect law-keeping is applied to the sinners account, causing him to be declared legally righteous. 2 Cor.5:21, Rom.3:24ff.

16. *True.* In justification, Jesus' perfect law-keeping is applied to the sinners account, and the sins of the sinner are placed on His, thereby being forgiven. 2 Cor.5:21.

17. *True.* God is holy and just, and must declare sinners guilty of breaking His law since they are guilty. He must punish those found guilty and He pours out His just wrath against them. To be made right with God, His wrath must be satisfied. When Jesus hung on the cross, God poured out His just wrath on Him as Jesus took on our sin and was punished by the Father in our place. Is.53, Rom.4:24f.

18. *False.* The perfect law-keeping of Christ alone placed on the sinners account is the legal basis for a sinner's justification. After justification and adoption, the Holy Spirit lives in the believer producing good works for the pleasure of God the Father. Rom.5:17f.

19. *False.* The legal basis for a sinner's justification is the work of Christ alone imputed to his account. Rom.5:9.

20. *True.* The work of Christ alone is the basis of justification. Rom.3:24f.

21. *True.* After justification (logically, though not chronologically), a person is adopted by God as His child. Jn.1:12, Gal.4:4ff.

22. *True.* After justification and adoption, the Holy Spirit sanctifies (indwells) believers and enables them to more and more live for and be like Jesus Christ. Jn14:15ff, 1 Cor.6:19, 1 Pet.1:2.

23. *False.* We are to voluntarily cooperate with the Holy Spirit as He works in us. Rom.8:13ff, Gal.5:16ff, 1 Pet.1:13ff.

24. *False.* While in love for God after we are justified, we are to live more and more for Christ, but we can never be perfect in this life. 1 Jn.1:8, Phil.3:12.

25. *False.* Baptism holds no virtue in itself or through the one who administers it. Only Jesus' finished work guarantees salvation. Gal.6:14f, Phil.3:3ff.

26. *True.* Christ's works alone are pure and undefiled and acceptable to God. Phil.3:8f.

27. *False.* God keeps our salvation. Christ accomplished it and the Holy Spirit applies it such that it can never be taken away. We obey God not to keep our salvation, but because we love Him and want to please Him. Rom.8:31ff, Phil.1:6.

28. *True.* A disciple belongs to God through Christ and loves to offer obedience to Him because of love. Rom.3:28, Jms.2:26.

29. *True.* Jesus said that if we love Him, we keep His commands. John 14:15ff.

30. *True.* A Christian loves to please God by obeying His Word. 1 Jn.2:3-6

AND THIS IS THE TESTIMONY, THAT GOD GAVE US ETERNAL LIFE, AND THIS LIFE IS IN HIS SON.

WHOEVER HAS THE SON HAS LIFE; WHOEVER DOES NOT HAVE THE SON OF GOD DOES NOT HAVE LIFE.

I WRITE THESE THINGS TO YOU WHO BELIEVE IN THE NAME OF THE SON OF GOD,

THAT YOU MAY KNOW THAT YOU HAVE ETERNAL LIFE.

1 JOHN 5:11-13

NOTES/REFLECTIONS

APPENDIX

RESOURCES WE RECOMMEND

BELOW IS A SHORT LIST OF RESOURCES THAT WILL BE USEFUL TO YOU TO GROW IN YOUR LOVE AND KNOWLEDGE OF GOD.

1. The Reformation Study Bible (NKJV or ESV). The excellent study notes and included materials will help you more fully understand the Word

2. Big Truths for Young Hearts - Bruce Ware. This is a beginning systematic theology or summary of Christian doctrine. These topical truths will be the grounding for your Devotional Commentary. We have written a study guide that you can use to help you. It can be found at www.legacydiscipleship.org.

3. Manual of Christian Doctrine by Louis Berkoff (not the Summary of Christian Doctrine. This is an introductory volume that will lay a foundation of truth that you will build upon for the rest of your life.

4. Valley of Vision – A Collection of Puritan Prayers and Devotions edited by Arthur Bennett. These prayers will help guide your prayers as you grow in your conversation with God

5. A Praying Life- Paul Miller   A down-to-earth practical book assessing prayer, troubleshooting problems and giving practical advice on how to be intentional in this area of our Faith that is usually lagging. There is a study guide available.

6. Persuasions - Doug Wilson   This little book of conversations between a Christian and a non-Christian will grow your confidence and technique in talking about the things of God to others in a godly way. Each little part is three pages. There is a study guide available at www.legacydiscipleship.org.

YOU CAN FIND MORE RESOURCES TO HELP YOU IN YOUR GROWTH IN DISCIPLESHIP AT WWW.LEGACYDISCIPLESHIP.ORG

www.ingramcontent.com/pod-product-compliance
Lightning Source LLC
Chambersburg PA
CBHW081437090426
42740CB00017B/3343